Stories with Connie

The Little Book of Attributes
for Student Entrepreneurs

By Marc Steren and Tami Levey

The Little Book of Attributes
for Student Entrepreneurs

Copyright © 2018 Marc Steren and Tami Levey

All rights reserved.

No part of this book may be reproduced by any means, electronic or mechanical, without permission in writing from the publisher.

DEDICATION

I was away when I heard of Connie Giles' passing. She was a mentor, colleague and most of all, a friend. I think she would be comforted to know that 100% the proceeds of this book will go to her favorite cause, education.

This book has Connie as the storyteller but these stories are from real entrepreneurs, and these stories are theirs. Connie is to the book what she was to me and to many of her students and colleagues, a guide.

Marc Steren & Tami Levey

CONTENTS

Introduction	1
Purpose	3
Learning Through Questions	7
Grit	11
Simple is the Focus	13
Givers	15
Timing	17
Optimism	19
What Risk	21
The Struggle is Your Friend	23
Reflection	25
The Science and Tactics For the Attributes	27

INTRODUCTION

It was my second year teaching entrepreneurship at the Bullis School. Before Bullis, I had never been a teacher. I was an entrepreneur. I am an entrepreneur. My first year in the classroom seemed to go off without a hitch. The students had been broken into 5 teams and each had come up with a viable entrepreneurial concept. One team, Kanga Trash and Energy Systems, had developed a trash bag that could be retrofitted into stadium seats so that in lieu of throwing trash on the floor, the fan could easily dispose of their trash right at their seats. Kanga had even been able to sign up a few stadiums to use their breakthrough product and had maintained momentum and worked on their concept post high school graduation and while in college.

But during my second year, I struggled. Whatever worked the year before fell flat with the current crop of students.

One morning after an especially tough class, I found myself in the office of Connie Giles. Connie was the k-12 director of curriculum, and a first for Bullis. Connie broke the glass ceiling to become the first African American to hold her prestigious position, and she had boundless energy. Prior to joining Bullis, it was Connie who I collaborated with and she helped me design the curriculum. I would send her pages of ideas and lessons, and she would send the pages back to me, marked up and filled with feedback. There was always feedback.

Connie was my mentor and the person to whom I turned whenever I found myself in a conundrum. And on that day, I was discouraged.

"They just don't get it," I said to Connie, feeling exasperated. She peered at me from behind her glasses.

"And whose fault is that?" She asked me pointedly as she closed the book she had been reading before I entered her office. With her response, any sentiment of feeling sorry for myself disappeared. I would go back to the drawing board and continue to work with my students, remembering a simple phrase, "If the kids don't get it, whose fault is it? Mine."

To be honest, that class which felt so difficult for me may or may not have been the best class I have ever taught, but rest assured, they went on to achieve as much success as the class before them and each class after them.

I thanked her for input and started to head out of the door. Her message that self-pity would not be tolerated was metaphorically ringing in my ears.

"XYZ" she said as I started to leave her office.

"XYZ, what does that mean?" I asked.

"Your fly is open," and with that she reopened her book and directed her attention away from me.

Before walking out, I turned back quickly to ask her, "do you mind if I come back next week?"

"Sure," she said. And that's how my stories with Connie began.

PURPOSE

After the previous week's conversation, I checked to be sure my fly was zippered before entering Connie's office. We decided to meet weekly, but now that I was here, I wasn't quite sure what to expect.

She told me that this was going to be our first of 9 weeks together. Each week, she would tell me a story. What I did with that story and how I shared it with my students was going to be left up to me.

"Stories are meant to be shared," she said, "but how and when you share these stories I will leave to your discretion." I anticipated staying about ten minutes. All of Connie's stories tended to be direct and to the point and most of all, short.

Before I knew it, Connie was into her first story:

Michael O'Neil was a Georgetown University student powering his way through a dual degree, a master's in business administration and a law degree. After classes, he would hop on the Whitehurst Freeway, blasting the music in his car with a sense of accomplishment that his day was complete. On one of these euphoric drives home, Michael felt a sharp pain rip through his side, but by the time he made it home the pain had subsided enough for him to forget it and head to class, per usual, the next day.

By later that week, the pain had morphed into a dull nuisance. Michael was able to ignore it for a bit but days later the sharp pain returned. This time, he couldn't simply wait it out so he took himself to Georgetown Hospital. While sitting in the waiting room, Michael wasn't too concerned. Between the days and nights of driving back and forth from Georgetown, add in the stress and excitement of planning a wedding, he thought his nerves were getting the best of him, or maybe an ulcer, at worst, due to his heavy schedule.

A battery of tests were ordered. The doctor grimaced as he approached Michael, probably one of many difficult conversations the doctor had given numerous times to various patients. As most doctors confess, this type of conversation never gets easier.

Michael had cancer. Specifically, a tumor the size of a baseball was growing inside of him. The actual diagnosis was non-Hodgkin's lymphoma. Michael was devastated, and the trajectory of his life changed the moment he heard the news.

Four rounds of chemotherapy was the prescribed treatment. With each round, Michael lost his hair and his strength, but that was not the worst of it.

Prior to his diagnosis, Michael had spent the past two years being active and busy; his life was constantly filled with everything from studying to exercising to finding adventures with his fiancé. He was a "go getter" and he felt as if he never had enough time in a day to get through everything. Now, that's all he had. The time was actually for his recuperation but regardless, it was time to be alone, time to be with his thoughts. His loneliness and isolation led to depression. Even with his loved ones' support, he had a difficult time seeing his way out of the circumstances in which he was living.

Michael's energy had always propelled him, it was a force that he never cultivated or appreciated until it had been torn from him. Before his illness, Michael had always felt like he controlled his own destiny. But here, alone in his hospital bed, Michael felt powerless. Powerless to control who he was. As he spoke to other patients in the hospital, he realized that they felt the same way. They all shared feelings of loneliness and boredom, and complained about *the lack of control* they felt. During one of these lonely nights he woke up with a realization: while he could not control the spread of his cancer, he could control his health care plan. Each patient, in fact, could have control over their own health care plan. Michael realized they were not each alone. He discovered he had a purpose and from that realization GetwellNetwork was born.

GetwellNetwork is a healthcare company with a purpose to transform the one-size-fits-all approach to the patient/doctor relationship. Getwell seeks to connect the proper information to the proper provider so that personal engagement and cross-continuum solutions can be delivered. The goal of the company is to empower patients and clinicians so that healthy outcomes are derived.

The desire Michael had to revolutionize the healthcare experience was largely based upon his own battle with cancer. Michael found the first step in what we have coined *the purpose curve*. The purpose curve derives initially from an idea, a spark, a trigger of sorts to make a change. This trigger, then, must be turned into action. Action drives the project to deliver on more and propels the continuation of action. The third part of the purpose curve equation is the most critical, as it is the motivation that initiated you to act. The next logical step is to question if others will share in that purpose.

Let's go back to Michael's story to see if he was able to share his purpose and if others wanted to be part of that vision.

In the early stages of GetwellNetwork, the company was always short on cash. As any entrepreneur will tell you, cash is king but especially so during the early stage of the venture. In fact, GetwellNetwork was so low on cash that the company only had $17,000 in the bank. The bigger problem was that payroll was coming on Friday. And to make payroll, Michael needed $19,000. He gathered his employees and broke the news over lunch.

"Folks," he said, holding the paychecks and slowly passing them out. But the employees already knew. One by one, they came up to Michael and handed back their paycheck. "The company needs the cash more than I do," was the refrain from his employees. Only one person kept the paycheck as he was expecting a baby and his growing family needed the money. And so it became a tradition that every payroll they would gather at the lunch table and ask, "who needs a paycheck?" Those with a mortgage due or a big payment coming up would cash their checks but the rest of the team would throw their checks back in the pile.

The day would soon come when each employee would get their paychecks without fear of overdrawing, and then some. But for these employees, many of whom still work at GetwellNetwork today, they had earned so much more than money. They had joined Michael's purpose curve.

Connie closed her eyes, and pressed her hands over her face. She got up from behind her desk and walked slowly to her whiteboard. She drew a curve with a radius and axis and wrote "The Purpose Curve." It looked something like this:

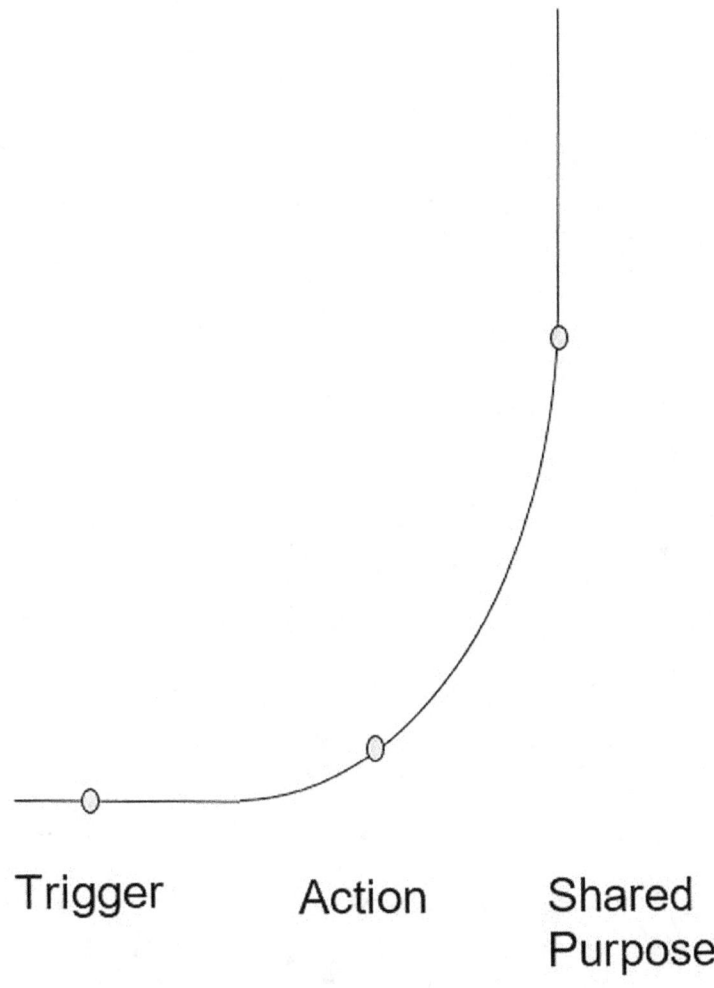

She placed the marker back into the holder. I had so many questions racing through my brain, for example, how do I apply the purpose curve to my class? To my life? But before I could ask a single question Connie sat back down and said, "Will I see you again the same next time week?" It was stated more than asked, and I knew my time with her was over for now.

"Yes," I said as I picked up my notebook and left. On my walk back to my classroom, I just kept thinking about the purpose curve and could feel my growing anticipation for our next meeting together.

LEARNING THROUGH QUESTIONS

A week had passed since my first conversation with Connie. I saw her here and there around campus and realized that I felt different, awkward, almost as if the story she shared with me was somehow confidential. While slightly apprehensive about our next meeting, I was hoping to be just as inspired as I had been by our last encounter.

I nearly flew into her office and plopped myself down in the chair without so much as a hello.

"Nice to see you too," she said from behind her desk, composed as ever, going through her articles. "Shall we begin?" I merely nodded, a bit disheveled but with my notebook in hand, I pulled out my pen.

"Ok," she said, "I will take that as a yes," and she began her next story:

Learning through questions she wrote on the whiteboard.

When people tease Norm Augustine with the old joke, "what are you, a rocket scientist?" he is one of the few people who can answer, "yes!" A rocket engineer by trade, he almost didn't go to college. His high school teacher noticed that he was performing well in school, especially in math and science, and asked where he was applying.

Norm laughed it off as no one from his family had attended college. He didn't see college as an option and therefore had never given it any serious thought. His teacher handed him a pamphlet with a college name on it and asked, "have you heard of this one?"

The front cover said two words, Princeton University. Norm claims that since he had heard of it, he went ahead and applied. To his surprise, he got in and decided to become a park ranger. But the major didn't quite click with him and one day while on a train home from class he struck up a conversation with someone he knew who also attended Princeton. That person was always doing neat things so Norm decided to ask him what his major was, and was told aerospace engineer. Hmm, sounded pretty cool. When Norm went back to Princeton he changed his major to become an aerospace engineer.

Norm Augustine would flourish in both the public and private domain. He went on to serve in two presidential administrations and eventually would serve as the Secretary of the Army. But his love, ever since he changed his major to aerospace engineer, was space and the shuttles that would test the limits of science fiction and reality. His dream of designing a space shuttle would come true as part of Lockheed Martin, a pioneer company in the aerospace industry. Norm became the CEO of Lockheed Martin, overseeing 17 acquisitions where he transformed the company from having a $4 billion revenue to $44 billion.

Norm, it appeared, had all the answers. In 1980, NASA contracted with Lockheed Martin to build its newest space shuttle. Since the shuttles traveled through space everything was measured to the most minute detail, including the weight of the space shuttle. This is where the problems began. The NASA specifications required that the fuselage weigh a certain weight. The Lockheed Martin fuselage that Norm oversaw was 2,000 pounds over the specification. Norm's team of engineers were able to cut that weight by 1200 pounds but they were still 800 pounds away from their target.

Norm felt like his team had to be missing something. They had been working day and night and yet they still couldn't cut the necessary 800 pounds. He brought his teams out to look at the space shuttle still parked on the ground.

It was amazing to look at, painted in its recognizable black and white, distinct even when miles away from Earth. The team discussed ideas but nothing seemed to click.

A young engineer working on Norm's team asked a seemingly unimportant question about the design,

"Why is the space shuttle white?"

No one, including Norm, understood why this question had any relevance.

"All space shuttles are painted white," someone else from the team responded.

The young engineer was asking the question, however, because it related directly to the weight issue they were facing. Did the shuttle *have* to be painted white? How much did the paint weigh once applied to the fuselage? As it turned out, the paint was weighing the vessel down, to the tune of 800 pounds. The plans, without the paint, were accepted and NASA was able to successfully launch the space shuttle.

According to Norm, this story served as a real reminder of the importance of asking questions. He realized that somewhere along his career he had himself stopped asking questions, and was so grateful for the young engineer's curiosity. Norm believed his age and experience gave him all of the answers already, but was instantly reminded by his younger and much less experienced team member of the value of asking questions.

Connie's story about Norm and being inquisitive reminded Connie of another great entrepreneur, Patricia Henriques. Patricia "Pat" was an adventurer and shared an important lesson as to what makes a great entrepreneur.

As a young college graduate, just 22 years old and with only $800 in her pocket, Pat headed to Paris. It was a dream of hers to see the cathedrals of Paris and eat its world renown cuisine. Dreams soon turned to reality as after just a few short weeks in Paris, Pat found that she was nearly broke. Though she had a job working at a boutique, it was not enough to cover the high cost of living in Paris. She therefore budgeted each week for groceries.

Pat had taken French in college and believing she was fluent went to the market to order her favorite delicacy, one pork chop as an end of the week treat for herself. She had carefully budgeted for this and was looking forward to her delicious meal. After placing her order in French, the butcher asked her a follow-up question, in French. Pat did not understand the question but being too proud to ask for clarification, merely nodded her head in the affirmative.

Rather than be charged for a single pork chop, Pat ended up unwittingly agreeing to purchase the entire pork roast, which cost her her entire week's grocery budget. This simple interaction, and her unwillingness to ask for clarification on the butcher's question taught Pat a life-long lesson that she now lives by and preaches to others: always ask questions.

Clarifications, asking "what if" and "why do we do it this way" are questions that every entrepreneur needs to be asking themselves.

Pat's desire to learn and her unabashed questions since that time have led her to many successes. As chairman and founder of Management Alternatives, she led the firm's 20 year growth from start-up to national leader in corporate relocation services. After successfully exiting the company, she founded the Henlee Group, advising and coaching entrepreneurs in emerging and high growth companies.

It is evident that asking questions, getting clarification, and exposing your curiosity can only help in entrepreneurial endeavors. Even the experts don't know it all so go ahead, and bravely participate by asking your question; there really is no wrong question to ask.

Marc Steren & Tami Levey

GRIT

Week 3 with Connie couldn't come fast enough. I had been spending the last two weeks trying to figure out "why" I was teaching. Every day, whenever I found myself struggling, I came back to the why and it seemed to help me focus. To be honest, I felt as if I had more energy. There was more energy to start the day and at the end of each day, I found myself reflecting on the reason for each lesson.

I also began asking more questions. I assumed less and asked more. Interestingly enough, those I was asking questions to seemed more interested in the conversation. I really felt like I was getting somewhere. I entered her office.

Connie was behind her desk and began as usual by slowly putting her reading down and getting right to her story:

Peter Barris moved around a lot as a child. It was difficult for him to make and keep friends, and he claims he never felt like he quite fit in. Peter recalled a time, however, when as a high-schooler all of that changed.

As the new kid in Youngstown, Ohio, Peter felt like this particular relocation his family made was the worst one yet for him. The other students were merciless with their teasing and Peter found he just didn't want to take it anymore. Then, the last straw for Peter happened. One of the biggest kids in the school, a starting player on the basketball team, slammed all of his books on Peter's desk and demanded that his homework be finished by 3:00, the end of the school day. Peter had had enough. He threw the other boy's books off his desk, and stood toe-to-toe with someone a good foot and half taller than himself. Not really eyeball-to-eyeball, Peter clenched his fists and was ready for what he thought would come next.

The punch that Peter was anticipating never came. Instead, the basketball player patted Peter on the shoulder, collected his books from the floor, and left Peter alone. Then, the most unexpected thing happened - Peter and the "basketball bully" became friends, a friendship that he still maintains to this day.

Years later, Peter found himself again in an intimidating situation. It was the interview of a lifetime for Peter because he was meeting with Jack Welch. At the time, Jack Welch was a division head and a well-respected member of the General Electric team though he would eventually become the most decorated CEO of General Electric, putting the company on the map. Under Jack Welch's tenure, GE's company value rose 4,000% and he is now a celebrated businessman, author, and veritable leadership guru.

When Mr. Welch interviewed Peter he wasn't CEO at the time, however many within GE realized that he was a rising star and wanted to be placed on his team. Peter, a graduate of Northwestern, had the right experience for the new position Mr. Welch was seeking to fill, but previously he had only hired graduates from Harvard and Yale. Peter had been consulting for GE for the past several months and knew his interview was probably going to be more of a courtesy interview than anything else.

Mr. Welch had a disdain for consultants and as the interview began, Mr. Welch let Peter know right away what he thought of them. Peter was insulted. He had spent the last 6 months busting his ass for the company and he was going to let Mr. Welch know it. So he did.

Instead of backing down, Peter articulated point by point how much value he added to GE over the last 6 months, how indispensable he had become, and how much of an idiot Jack Welch would be to hire someone else for the job.

Peter left the interview feeling his chances of being hired were basically zero, but he was ok with that because he had stood up for himself and stood his ground. He remembered back to the day when those school books were shoved onto his desk and knew he would always stand up for himself, and let the chips fall where they may.

To Peter's surprise, he got the call the next day from Mr. Welch offering him the position. Mr. Welch said he was so impressed by Peter's ability to stand up for himself, and noted that GE needed more people like Peter Barris. The two worked together, and Peter insists that their relationship was perhaps one of the most influential in his lifetime thus far.

Fast forwarding through his impressive resume, Peter went on to become Chairman and General Partner for NEA, one of the world's largest and most active venture capital firms. He has been listed several times to the Forbes Midas List of top technology investors. In addition to sitting on many private and public companies' boards, he is also a founding member of a philanthropic organization in the Washington, DC area, Venture Philanthropy Partners.

Peter reflects back on both of the memories shared above, the homework incident and the interview with Jack Welch, as evidence of how we can truly be in control of our own destiny. He refuses to be intimidated by others, and believes that his moral compass has set him on the path to be true to himself, no matter who may be seated across the table.

As entrepreneurs you will no doubt face powerful people who may dismiss your value or your ideas entirely. Stand up to those who may bully you because in business, just as in life, there will be those who will always stand in your way. Find your path, stay true to yourself, and persist.

Not everyone is forced to do someone else's homework, but we all may be faced with similar struggles. How then, do you strengthen your grit to stand up for yourself?

SIMPLE IS THE FOCUS

I went to Connie's office for our weekly meeting and she wasn't there, which was strange. Connie never missed work. I leaned over her desk and saw her usual plethora of books and magazines. On top of one the magazines was a notepad. The first few words were in bold print:

Simple is the Focus

I turned to the next page and saw Connie had left me a note. "Marc, I am not feeling well today, so here is the next lesson. I hope you enjoy it."

Norm Augustine always bemoaned the tedious nature of due diligence during the acquisition process. This process refers to the reasonable steps taken by a person or company in order to satisfy a legal requirement when considering buying or selling something. Though a veteran of over 17 acquisitions, he never got used to the due diligence phase. Norm considered it a necessary evil of doing business. Towards the end of his tenure, he confided to his friend Warren about the trials and tribulations, as he saw it, of the long and exhausting process called due diligence.

Warren merely shrugged his shoulders, because as it turned out Warren had recently finished a multimillion dollar acquisition of a pipeline company.

The due diligence process had taken two days.

"How," asked Norm, "did you get through the business profile so quickly to determine if the project was right for you?"

"Simple," replied Warren. "It is a pipeline company. I had to find out the answer to one question, if the oil coming out of the ground is getting to the customer on time."

Every other factor was secondary. Warren simplified the entire process to focus on the single most important factor. When he determined that the product got to the customers, he knew it was the right venture.

Upon pressing Norm further as to who this mysterious Warren was, Norm laughed and said,

"That's easy, Warren Buffett."

Upon reflection, it makes sense that Warren is "Warren Buffett." Warren Buffett is the American investor, business magnate, CEO, and philanthropist. But it all started to come together. Throughout his career, simplicity has been the single core principle Warren Buffett adheres to, in fact, he's purchased 17 companies on .25 cents to the dollar, but sold off other parts if they complicated the simplicity of the business venture.

That is the brilliance of Warren Buffett. Simple, streamlined, focused.

Often when young entrepreneurs come up with an idea, they look for the "wow" factor, or some crazy new product to entice consumers to make a purchase. Companies come and go because in their effort to look big, they often miss out on the small, or simplest ideation of the product.

GIVERS

"What are we doing together, here in my office?" Connie asked me. I felt a little confused by the question.

"Learning," I answered, "I am certainly learning from you."

"Yes, that is part of it. But what we are doing together, here in my office each week, is I am giving you something." I saw her point. She was giving me something intangible, something I knew I wouldn't be able to value or appreciate immediately.

"Givers change the world," Connie told me as she looked out the window.

Fiona Macaulay is a giver.

Fiona Macaulay's mother worked on a Native American reservation for over thirty years as a researcher. She insisted that the Native Americans be a part of the research rubric. A common idea today, but at the time it was a revolutionary concept. Fiona's mother instilled in her a fierce independent streak but also the notion that we are here to serve others, not ourselves.

Sometimes as parents, we get more than we bargain for. Fiona, by the age of 17, left home to seek a job and find herself in the world. Taking her mother's lessons to heart, Fiona discovered that you only find yourself in the service of others.

By her mid-20's, Fiona was backpacking through South Africa where she toured a museum in Johannesburg dedicated to the struggles of Apartheid. According to Fiona, there was a small sign in the window looking for an intern to work for free. While having no resume, Fiona wrote out her name and qualifications on a piece of paper and submitted it for the job. She was immediately "hired." As an intern, she noticed the eagerness of young children engaged in one particular computer game at the museum. The computer game was part of a software program that taught children basic educational skills. After backpacking through much of Africa, Fiona knew that this was something the children of Africa desperately needed.

At the time, South Africa had a severe shortage of teachers, and even fewer textbooks, desks, and schools. Fiona was convinced that this computer software program at the museum could help fill the need in greater Johannesburg. Fiona sought out the director of the museum to share her vision of expansion for this educational tool and pitched her idea to the museum director. The director was clear: she didn't have the time to explore other uses for the software. Met with opposition to her idea, Fiona asked if she could license the software herself, to which she was given a surprising "yes." With no experience running a software company, let alone in a foreign country, Fiona was off and running. She was able to overcome her fear of being a first time entrepreneur with the solid belief that she would be serving others.

Once she obtained the licensing, Fiona set out to put this educational tool into the hands of every school, not just in Johannesburg, but in all of South Africa.

With her objective set before her, her aim to serve others in low income communities around the globe, Fiona took off. Her persistence, grit, and fearless independence allowed her to approach people, ask for meetings, and network. Fiona would drag her 'storyboard' of her software platform to anyone who would listen. She faxed potential client after potential client until finally, someone answered. She was able to secure the Peace Corps as a client. With just this single client in hand, and by keeping her focus on giving to others, Fiona managed to change the world.

By 26 years old, Fiona founded Making Cents, an international development firm which offered products and services in 50 countries, across Sub-Saharan Africa, the Middle East, and North Africa. It was her desire to improve education and her laser-like goal to serve others that drove her to her first of many successes. By the age of 35, Fiona founded a social venture, Youth Economic Opportunities Network, a global platform to strengthen entrepreneurship education and youth leadership development, with a focus on food security and nutrition for the world's youth population. In 2017, Fiona founded Powerhouse Women with the goal of helping others find their value and worth in the world, this time focusing on assisting women master 3 core skills: communicating, negotiating, and creating a holistic vision for themselves. Her work has remained "other-centric," and she serves as a guiding light for entrepreneurs who, like her, wish to give back through entrepreneurial endeavors.

Fiona's most basic tenant for her entrepreneurial endeavors has always been to serve others. According to Fiona, "You can be the most passionate person in the world but if you don't serve others, you serve nobody."

Serving others can mean something different to each person, so long as it always means adding value to your potential consumer's life.

TIMING

"Timing is everything," Connie began. "I wish I had met you ten years ago," she said with a hint of remorse in her voice. Connie appeared weaker each session that we met. She had begun to tire and I could tell that an illness was taking its toll on her.

She appeared frail. She was wearing a headscarf and I was uncertain if it was to cover the side effects of potential chemotherapy, or merely for style. I didn't ask.

"Is there anything I can get you?" I asked, but knew she would never take me up on my offer.

"Oh stop that, will you?" she said, then gave me a little smile. "It's a little stuffy in here, do you mind walking with me?"

We opened the doors to the outside and the sun beamed down on both of us. The fresh air and warmth of the sun immediately lifted both of our spirits. She closed her eyes and drew in a deep breath. "You never know what you have until it's gone," she said to no one in particular. Then she turned her attention to me and her next story,

"Timing is the next lesson."

In 1993, Michael Jordan was the king of the basketball world. He had just won a three-peat championship, the first since the 1960's Boston Celtics. Michael Jordan wasn't just the king of the basketball world, but of the shoe world as well. Everyone wanted to be like Mike and wear his Nike's Jordan high tops.

Around the same time, Seth Berger had developed a hip brand, AND1, with its own high tops. They had just managed to enter 10 Foot Lockers as a test run for their shoes. It was the big break Seth had been waiting for, but matched up against the "Jordan's" his AND1 shoes didn't stand a chance.

Then the strangest thing happened - Michael Jordan retired from basketball and decided to play baseball instead. What young basketball player wanted to wear basketball shoes from a baseball player? The timing was perfect for AND1 and their shoes took off in sales. Within a year, Seth Berger and AND1 has a distribution deal in thousands of Foot Locker stores.

Seth explains, "If I had waited to sell to Foot Locker 6 months later it would have been too late and some other shoe company would have seen the opportunity and filled the void. A year earlier, and we simply couldn't compete against the Jordan brand. A key to all great entrepreneurs is seeing the opportunity and knowing when that timing is right," said Seth.

His company AND1 had revenues of $1.7 million in their first year, and Seth sold the company in 2005 when AND1's revenues were around their peak of about $250 million. Currently, Seth coaches basketball at a private school outside of Philadelphia, right where he began his company. He claims that there is no such thing as failure in entrepreneurial endeavors, only pivoting. His success with AND1 was ultimately driven by his ability to read the market and make the right product at the right time.

OPTIMISM

Connie smiled at me as I walked into her office.

"This is a topic I know you are going to like," she said to me as she slowly took off her glasses. She had looked like she was going to stand up but decided against it.

"Optimism, my friend, optimism. That will be the story for today."

Shirish Pareek was born in Kanpur, India, to lower middle class parents who made education a priority. Shirish's hard work, good grades, and high test scores won him admittance to the prestigious Indian Institute of Technology where he began his career as a mechanical engineer. Despite being off to this strong start, Shirish always had an eye for coming to America. He knew this was where opportunity called, and where his future successes would be met. When he told his parents he was heading to the United States, his parents asked a simple question, "You are doing so well here, why do you want to go to United States? How do you know you will succeed there?"

"I just know," Shirish responded with an optimism that would not be deterred.

With an acceptance letter from Carnegie Mellon University in hand, Shirish came to America and continued his education. He took a night job in a metal factory and says he fell in love with the American manufacturing industry. At only 25 years old, Sirish finished school and felt it was time to start his own company.

Shirish became the founder, President and CEO of Hydraulex Global. Today, Hydraulex Global is the largest United States manufacturer of hydraulic parts and equipment. It is a $90 million corporation that operates worldwide. In a nutshell, Hydraulex Global takes machinery that would otherwise be heaped into landfills and "brings it back to life."

Shirish is constantly working to help the manufacturing industry in the United States and is currently raising funds in an effort to set up manufacturing nodes and apprenticeships so that the innovation of manufacturing remains constant. He sees his role as an entrepreneur as one of a responsibility to others, namely to create jobs for others within the industry. His world view and optimism has led him in a variety of directions. While many saw manufacturing as a dead industry, Shirish's belief and optimism in the industry has been rewarded. Since the end of 2016, the United States has added close to 300,000 new manufacturing jobs.

As Connie finished her story, she reflected for a moment.

"What do you have to be grateful for?" she asked me.

"So much," I responded.

"'So much' is right, but what *specifically* do you have to be grateful for?"

"My kids," I answered immediately.

"And what about your kids can you be grateful for?"

"That they are happy," I struggled to verbalize my gratitude.

She looked at me cautiously, as if I still didn't understand. "That's true, happiness is important, but what are the things that make them happy?" She was clearly digging to get to some deeper, more meaningful response.

Before I could answer she beat me to it: "that they are healthy and that they live everyday with joy and optimism. Kids are still optimistic that everyday can be…" she hesitated for a moment, "fun," she concluded.

"You need to have an inner joy and the optimistic perspective that life is an adventure, that it can be awesome, that *you* are awesome and that we can make it better for everyone that comes into your life."

I knew instinctively that what she was saying was true. Life could be so much more consequential if only I could be more optimistic.

"I'm dying" she said. I had heard rumors about her health and had noticed she was wearing headscarves, but it was more than that. She seemed so tired.

"I'm so sorry" I said. I wished I had better words to comfort her but that is all that I could think of to say.

"Don't be. Make each day count. Be optimistic and make a difference."

WHAT RISK

The next week that I met with Connie, I could see the difference. Maybe I was just more attuned to it but every move she made seemed so much more deliberate, as if she couldn't afford to waste any of her energy.

"People play it so safe," she said. "They say they will do it tomorrow, always tomorrow. Or they are told by friends that something is too risky and are advised to do it later when they are more secure in life, whatever that means. Let me tell you something, there may not be a tomorrow for you, certainly there is not a tomorrow for me. My suggestion is to see the biggest risk of all as not taking the risk . Only those who never try anything never make mistakes. Take risks…"

Trenor Williams, a successful doctor and head of the family practice at Mammoth Hospital in California, seemed lost. He looked around his office and asked himself, "is this it, is this what I have to offer?" While most people would see his position as the pinnacle of success, Trenor recalls only his adverse feelings of no longer impacting patients' lives.

"I walked into my boss's office, shook his hand, and told him I was moving back east." Trenor did not have a job lined up, but knew he had to wait for his idea to provide better access for medical services to percolate in his brain. He supported himself as a bartender while he worked on his next step.

Today, Trenor keeps a white doctor's coat hanging in his office as a reminder of what helping his patients meant to him as he started his medical career. As a founder of Clinovations, a health-care strategy consulting firm which he later sold for millions of dollars, he has become a national leader in the healthcare provider sector. Currently, Trenor is heavily involved in the entrepreneurial ecosystem and nonprofit sector, and sits on the board for several companies.

With regard to his first move, from west coast to east coast, from head of a hospital to a bartender, Trenor claims that the notion he could face failure, or that his move was even a risk, never really entered into his lexicon of thinking, "I knew that if I worked hard and met the right people that I would make things work. I didn't necessarily have a clear picture of what that meant, but I knew that doing nothing and being unhappy was a lot riskier than making that move."

Another compelling story about taking risk involves Elana Fine. As a stay at home mom looking for some volunteer work to keep her busy and sane, Elana answered an advertisement. Five short years later, she is the current managing director of the Robert H. Smith School of Business Dingman Center for Entrepreneurship at the University of Maryland. It wasn't her first time taking a chance, and her risks have largely been met with success.

One of her first jobs in Boston was for an equity firm. She joined the company knowing it couldn't pay her a salary, but she took the position anyway. Elana says it was her belief in herself and the company that allowed her to take the risk and work without fully knowing how and when she would be paid. It was the right choice for her, and the risk was met with reward.

Now, in her work with student entrepreneurs, Elana's goal is to help students assess risks. She has identified that one of the biggest challenges that student entrepreneurs face is that startups can rarely pay market rates, and that many students therefore have to forgo opportunities to take paying jobs, even if that means delivering pizza. She helps direct students to organizations that look to fund students, and addresses the risks associated with their models in an effort to get their plans selected for funding.

Entrepreneurs are not foolish, and they do recognize the risk of making a change or taking that metaphorical leap, but their innate ability to assess risk differently often leads to the rewards we generally associate with them. Betting on themselves, and seeing opportunities where others might see dead ends is yet another common characteristic of entrepreneurs. That being said, just as it is important to plan for a rainy day by having an umbrella handy, so too is it important for entrepreneurs to have a plan B in place in case plan A does not come to fruition.

Success stories are littered with examples of modern legends who took great leaps of faith, think of Bill Gates, Steve Jobs, and Mark Zuckerberg - all of whom dropped out of college to pursue their dreams of changing the world in some way. But don't kid yourself, not every successful entrepreneur is a name or a brand you will recognize.

THE STRUGGLE IS YOUR FRIEND

"Today is my last day at Bullis. I simply don't have the strength to come in anymore."

I wanted to object, to tell her that she could do it, but one look at Connie revealed it all. She was so skinny. It was clear that the cancer was eating away at her from the inside. It was unbearable for me, but here she was, making the sacrifice to come to work so that she could impart her wisdom.

"If you keep looking at me like that I am gonna smack you!" she teased. I smiled back at her.

"No need to waste time with needless salutations, let's begin."

Jonathon Perrelli gained his first client by hacking into the computer system of UUnet.

"Can't you see that you need network security?" he remembers telling them. Although not a strategy he would endorse today, it certainly made a point at the time. Jonathon wasn't always so brash. In fact, much of his early school years were full of struggle. His teachers thought he wouldn't add up to much. He couldn't sit still. As an adult Jonathon was diagnosed with ADHD but when he was a kid, the label was merely inept, incompetent, or worse.

It was Jonathon's ability to overcome his struggles that would later serve him well. In fact, he credits much of his creativity to his ability to see many things at once while others can only see a narrow and limited picture.

When I met with Jonathon to discuss his journey, he was sitting on the patio of his Reston, Virginia office wearing a LifeFuels t-shirt and working on his laptop. He, of course, couldn't stay seated for long. He got up, walked around, speaking and pointing in many directions as he began his story.

After struggling through school, Jonathon hoped to become a Marine in the United States Army and spent the last two years of college preparing himself physically for the challenges of becoming one. He stopped drinking beer, began a training regiment, and knew just where he would sign up. It was his dream, after all, and he was determined to make it a reality. After incurring a shoulder injury, Jonathon continued his training until it became clear that he would not pass the physical tests required. He watched his lifelong dream of becoming a Marine slip away. It was, however, the first time that Jonathon could stay focused on a long term goal and it was this singular ability of being able to focus on a long term goal which has provided Jonathon with the ability to pivot and shift his goals elsewhere.

It was yet another struggle that led Jonathon to his current venture, LifeFuels. Jonathon's wife was pregnant with their third child. It was more difficult for his wife, and for him as well, to maintain the "pristine" practices that couples often employ with their first pregnancy: eating organically, taking prenatals, etc. Life moves faster and doesn't always allow for the best laid plans when toddlers are involved. He found each night he would prepare a shake for his wife containing healthy nutrients to make sure that she stayed on top of the proper nutrition that she needed to have a healthy baby.

As many great entrepreneurs have found, Jonathon identified a need in the marketplace. In fact, his discovery exposed a void in the marketplace. He envisioned a bottle that did more than just measure ounces of water. He created a smart bottle that contains removable "fuel pods" so that each individual can mix and match nutrients, essentially creating their own personalized recipe within the smart bottle. The product empowers people to infuse their water with natural fruit enhanced flavors while delivering measurable fluids of vitamins and electrolytes. The product differs greatly from what the market currently offers in terms of sports drinks like Gatorade and Powerade.

There is a second reason that Jonathon founded LifeFuels. He had watched his mother drink diet soda for 30 years. He then watched her suffer and die of a horrible disease, cancer. He began to question whether or not she would have made the same choice to drink diet soda if she knew what she was actually ingesting and more importantly, if she would have chosen diet soda had there been a healthier and tastier option that she could have created for herself.

Despite Jonathon's early struggles as a student, he knew as an adult that learning must never stop. So how then does a creative ADHD adult absorb the learning? He knew his limitations, and he still couldn't sit for long period of times. He found the solution in Ted Talks. Ted Talks are informative videos that range between 5 and 20 minutes long, just the right amount of time for someone with ADHD. Jonathon believes the length of each Ted Talk keeps him focused and allows him to apply the daily lesson from each to his daily goals throughout the work day. When asked about how passionate he feels about his product, it was clear that his personal reasons for creating an innovative and healthy way to keep track of fluids - the life of his third child and death of his mother - keep him well connected to the purpose of his product.

In the past three years of work with LifeFuels, Jonathon admits to having missed 5 workdays where he felt unmotivated. His decision to stay home rather than work through the low feelings of motivation were simple: Jonathon did not want his employees to see him out of sorts, afraid that his mood might negatively affect their productivity.

As a way to show others that learning differently can be overcome, Jonathon mentors two people a year. Furthermore, he relies upon mentors himself in an effort to learn and grow and keep himself moving along the entrepreneurship ladder, both vertically and horizontally. Another tactic Jonathon employs to overcome his struggle with ADHD is his use of mind maps, or diagrams to visually organize information. This tool, which can show how each relationship or idea can be connected to the whole of the project, can help capture your thoughts and bring them to "visual life," another technique that he claims helps with his ADHD.

REFLECTION

I had come to the hospital for our last visit but I was not permitted into her room. Apparently and rightfully so, only family was allowed.

I felt rejected, sad and started to walk out of the hospital when a nurse approached me.

"Marc?"

"Yes," I responded.

"This is for you." It was a small piece of paper with one word on it. "Connie thought you might show up and wanted to make sure you received this. She said it would be your final lesson."

The paper had one word on it, "reflection." There was no story to go with it, but I went home that night to reflect. I have tried each evening since Connie's death to reflect on the stories she shared with me, on her 9 lessons. I ask myself: did I live today with purpose, did I overcome? Have I attempted to serve others? I try to live each day with the notion that it could be my last. I am thankful for my time with Connie and am supremely grateful for the wisdom that she shared with me.

I know that I can say with certainty, as I reflect back to our weekly meetings, that I have learned from Connie. I hope the lessons shared here can impact you just as much as they have impacted me.

THE SCIENCE AND TACTICS FOR THE ATTRIBUTES

PURPOSE

The Science Behind Purpose

Purpose driven companies[1] report 3x annual revenues over their competitors. Simon Sinek's Start with Why[2] posits that purpose is *the* differentiator that propelled consumers to choose Apple products. Teams[3] in companies that share a common purpose score higher than their peers in productivity.

For individual employees, Deloitte recently conducted a study[4] in which 73% of employees in purpose driven fields felt engaged while only 23% in non-purpose driven companies felt the same engagement.

A question which many student entrepreneurs ask is, "what does a purpose driven company look like?" In Robert Quinn's article[5] in Harvard Business Review the author states, "Rally the organization behind an authentic higher **purpose**—an aspirational mission that explains how **employees** are making a difference and gives them a sense of meaning." In essence, purpose is a ***shared meaning*** that will have your employees more engaged and happier at work.

Monthly Goal Chart

Goal #1

Purpose:

Goal Question:

___

Goal #2

Purpose:

Goal Question:

___

Goal #3

Purpose:

Goal Question:

Weekly Goal Chart	Monday	Tuesday	Wednesday	Thursday	Friday	Accountability
Week 1 Goal:						
Week 2 Goal:						
Week 3 Goal:						
Week 4 Goal:						

How to use the Monthly Goal Chart:

Goals

1. A goal that you want to achieve this month
2. Statement is in present tense as if it is already achieved
3. Review the statement + say it morning and night
4. Must be measurable

Purpose

1. Why did you pick this goal

Goal Question

1. Always ask yourself when approached with a difficult question – "will this help me achieve my goal of ___".
   How to use the Weekly Goal Chart
   Write this 1 goal with an end objective at the end of the 4 weeks → ...
2. Underneath each week, write that smaller week's goal.
3. Under each day, write the measurement to determine the task of success, 2nd line is the actual task and 3rd line is a simple ✔ if completed.
   → Don't stop the chain!
4. Weekly accountability → make sure to reflect and discuss the week's activities without someone else + make necessary corrections.
5. Schedule the daily task into the Daily Schedule!

The Science Behind Questions as Learning

Research has determined that most conversations can serve two functions, likeability and learning. Asking questions serves both: when we tell stories to our conversational counterparts they like it and in turn like us for sharing, and as for the learning component, by asking questions, we will learn about the other person engaged in the conversation and by merely listening to them, you will be liked in return.

Most people don't grasp that asking a lot of questions unlocks learning and improves interpersonal bonding.

The ability to learn is tied to curiosity. Research goes on to explain:

Great learners retain this childhood drive, or regain it through another application of self-talk. Instead of focusing on and reinforcing initial disinterest in a new subject, they learn to ask themselves "curious questions" about it and follow those questions up with actions. Carol Sansone, a psychology researcher, has found, for example, that people can increase their willingness to tackle necessary tasks by thinking about how they could do the work differently to make it more interesting. In other words, they change their self-talk from This is boring to I wonder if I could...?

The lesson here is don't lose your childhood curiosity and continue to ask why. Conversations with questions allow you to ask, listen, learn and be liked. All are efforts that you will find bring you closer to your entrepreneurship goal.

LEARNING

The Question/ Learning Framework

How is it done now?	Why is it done this way?	What if we did this?	

But learning isn't just about asking questions, it's about experiencing something new. Larry Weinberg is founder of Bowa, a building and design company in the Greater Washington, DC area and Virginia. Although Larry started on a traditional path to learning and success, he veered from it early on and has never looked back.

Larry identifies himself as a lifelong learner, but also as a *different type* of learner then schools generally measure. Because he values experiences as well as education, Larry pulled his children from school for a year to "follow the sun," literally traveling the world to see other cultures in an effort to get and give his children a worldly education, one that cannot be obtained by sitting in a classroom. The experience was truly once-in-a-lifetime, and Larry said he and his family benefited enormously from their adventure. Learning from real experiences is quite different from reading about experiences, and Larry claims that theory and practice must meet in the real world.

The final piece in the question/learning framework is the experience. Gaining experience means you may need to venture beyond your comfort zone and stretch. New experiences will be the best way you for to learn.

The Science Behind Grit

Grit refers to your motivational drive, how much you inspire yourself, and your ability to sustain efforts towards long term goals.

Resilience refers to your optimism and ability to continue towards your stated goal in the face of failure. It is your ability to bounce back when a setback occurs.

Perseverance refers to your ability to see challenges as opportunities, not barriers.

According to an article published through the Positive Psychology Program website entitled *5 Ways to Develop a Growth Mindset Using Grit and Resilience* psychologists have come up with 5 basic ways you can acquire grit, resilience and perseverance:

1. **Your language choice**: Instead of declaring someone is a generic characteristic think of specific reasons that displays that trait. For example, instead of saying you are "so smart," instead say it is great that you knew to place the comma at the right place in the sentence structure.
2. **Hang out with the right people:** Surround yourself with people who stick with their goals and see their goals through to fruition. Jim Rohn[6] said you are the sum of your 5 closest friends that you spend the most time with. If you keep dogs as friends you wake up with fleas. Hang out with the right people that will push you and make you a better person.
3. Growth Mindset[7]: In Dweck's ground breaking research, she discovered that those who have "growth mindsets" and those that believe that traits of intelligence and ability to learn are fixed, limit their abilities to succeed. Instead, develop a growth mindset, with the knowledge that you can improve yourself.
4. **Goal setting**: It is important to set large, big hairy goals[8] but from there, set smaller, achievable goals for yourself so that you can meet them and stay motivated to reach the next one, until it develops into a habit[9].

5. **Reflection**: This HBR article[10] showed that reflection improves productivity at work. For some students though, many struggle with journal practice of reflections. Gretchen Rubin[11] has a great suggestion for this, just write a one sentence reflection.

The Experience Framework

How is it done now?	Why is it done this way?	What if we did this?	Experience it

The Science of Simple

In Made to Stick[12], Professors Dan and Cliff Heath sought to determine what were the best pitches, in essence, what type of pitch was able to capture our attention and keep it. One of the core components was the ability to make the message simple and relatable to the audience. In an effort to sound so "smart," presenters often lost the audience due to a less interesting and compelling presentation.

In an article[13] in Harvard Business Review, the authors conduct extensive research to determine the most effective way to market to potential customers. The finding is clear, make your message "simple."

Rather than pulling customers into the fold, marketers are pushing them away with relentless and ill-conceived efforts to engage. What do consumers want from marketers? ***Simplicity****.* (emphasis added)

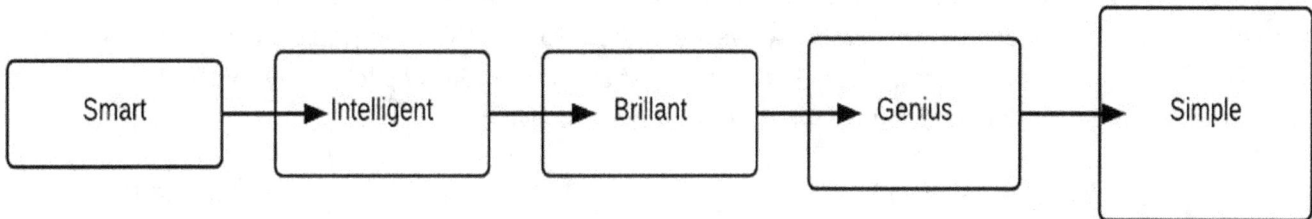

The above is Einstein's 5 levels of ascending Genius. To achieve genius, you must be able to filter your smart ideas to simple ones.

The Science Behind Giving

In Adam Grant's book, Give and Take[14], he discovers that there are 3 basic types of people at work:

1. Givers, those who will give their time and effort without looking for anything in return,
2. Takers, those who are looking to reap benefits without giving anything in return and
3. Reciprocity, those who will give if they know there is reciprocity down the road.

Interesting, those individuals who are most successful are the givers. Grant goes on to write:

Across occupations, if you examine the link between reciprocity styles and success, the givers are more likely to become champs.

In the end, the givers build stronger bonds with their co-workers, develop trust within the organization and tend to me more liked than their peers. So when the chance presents itself to just be nice and lend a hand, feel free to do so, you may just be helping your career.

The Giving Challenge

My young son Logan and I were in a shoe store, standing behind a mom and her young daughter at the register. The daughter was exhausted from shopping but was clearly excited by the idea of getting new shoes. The mom presented her credit card to the cashier, and the cashier swiped it at the point of sales. The cashier sheepishly handed the card back, as it had been denied.

"Um ma'am, the card came back as declined." The mother, clearly humiliated and disappointed, took back her credit card, took the new shoes box away from her daughter, and started to walk out of the store. Logan tugged at my shirt, "Dad, can't we do something?" In fact, we could. I asked the clerk to add the young girl's shoes to our bill. After the sale, the cashier handed one box to Logan and one to the young daughter. We grabbed our shoes and headed out the door. As we were about to exit, the young girl came running towards us and gave Logan a hug. The powerful nature of that hug made an enormous impact on my son, and it was contagious. We are now both constantly looking for moments of giving.

The idea of giving helps others, but just as importantly it will change how *you* feel. Giving opportunities don't have to be monetary, it just has to be selfless and in the pursuit of helping others. As an entrepreneurial challenge, we want you to plan a giving event, one that we call the 7 day giving challenge.

The Giving Challenge

Day	Giving Event	How did it make you feel

The Science Behind Optimism

In The Happiness Advantage[15], Shawn Achor provides a valuable insight, that happiness and optimism are a catalyst for success and not vice versa. Moreover, he elaborates that happiness can be learned. In addition, in Willpower Doesn't Work[16], optimism can be designed into your environment to help ensure success. These points are emphasized in the Blue Zone of Happiness[17] where environment and your attitude can help you live longer, happier lives.

The Science Behind Timing

It is difficult to time the perfect entry to a new market or the introduction of a new product. Therefore, successful companies and entrepreneurs turn to experiments[18].

Entrepreneurs have learned a lot from scientists and have even modeled their continuous innovation[19] after the scientific method. Experiments are structured to learn as quickly as possible without expending too many resources. In Running Lean[20], Ash Maurya defines a well-designed experiment as containing a few critical elements:

1. **Timebox**- there is a limited time for the experiment to occur
2. **Falsifiable**- Your hypothesis is either true or false at the end of the experiment
3. **Learning**- the experiment will yield as much learning as possible and will lead to an ascertainable decision after the experiment
4. **Control group**- though this is not included in Ash's rubric, it is always important to have a control group so you can compare to ensure that the experiment is having a causal effect.

Experiment Design

Before Experiment	After Experiment
Timebox- the time frame, typically anywhere from a week to 3 weeks	
Hypothesis that is falsifiable	True or False
Learning- what are you trying to learn from the experiment	What you actually learned
Control group in place	Comparative of control group and experiment
Next steps- as a result of the learning	Next Steps- I can now do X

The Science of Risk

The mythology that entrepreneurs throw caution to the wind is deeply embedded in Silicon Valley lore. These entrepreneurs seem to simply to drop everything to embark on an adventure that leads to riches. While this fallacy is perpetuated, it is, in fact, untrue. Great entrepreneurs don't pretend that there is no risk, simply that they acknowledge and assess risk differently. In this HBR article[21], the authors note that entrepreneurs aren't cowboys, just "methodical managers of risk." In other words, they learn to assess the risk and they are willing to act and take the risk, not disregard it. In Mastering Fear[22], the author instructs us that the very first thing in mastering fear is not to ignore it, but to acknowledge and decide to act to conquer it. Entrepreneurs are deciders who act despite the risk.

The Science of Overcoming Struggles

Society often still pegs those diagnosed with ADHD or ADD as difficult learners. In Learning how to learn[23], the breakthrough book by Barbara Oakley, she provides research which supports the notion that these learners can actually be more creative and may retain the information better than "normal" learners. In essence, Oakley argues that because people with ADHD don't have as strong a working memory, they need to work harder and therefor build stronger brain connections which in the end helps them learn and retain the information better. In addition, these learners are forced to make simpler, more elegant explanations of the learning which also helps them retain the information more easily.

Overcoming struggle is in fact difficult, but if we proceed with deliberate practice[24] and we practice difficult tasks just enough to stretch ourselves and receive expert feedback, we can, in fact, overcome struggles and get better.

FOOTNOTES

1. www.kornferry.com/institute/purpose-powered-success?reports-and-insights
2. https://startwithwhy.com/
3. https://www.amazon.com/Big-Potential-Transforming-Achievement-Well-Being/dp/1524761532
4. https://gethppy.com/employee-engagement/3-ways-purpose-driven-organizations-increase-employee-engagement
5. http://web.a.ebscohost.com/ehost/detail/detail?vid=7&sid=c2004e98-7c1a-4ad9-a4e2-58a837cb8060%40sessionmgr4010&bdata=JnNpdGU9ZWhvc3QtbGl2ZQ%3d%3d#AN=130332014&db=buh
6. https://www.businessinsider.com/jim-rohn-youre-the-average-of-the-five-people-you-spend-the-most-time-with-2012-7
7. https://www.amazon.com/Mindset-Psychology-Carol-S-Dweck/dp/0345472322
8. https://www.harpercollins.com/9780066620992/good-to-great
9. https://www.amazon.com/Habit-Stacking-Small-Changes-Minutes-ebook/dp/B00JQHB67O
10. https://hbr.org/2014/05/the-power-of-reflection-at-work
11. https://gretchenrubin.com/books/the-happiness-project/about-the-book/
12. https://www.amazon.com/Made-Stick-Ideas-Survive-Others/dp/1400064287
13. http://web.b.ebscohost.com/ehost/detail/detail?vid=5&sid=6d258dfc-0b0e-4846-818b-ec118d97cf6d%40sessionmgr101&bdata=JnNpdGU9ZWhvc3QtbGl2ZQ%3d%3d#AN=74458912&db=buh
14. https://www.amazon.com/Give-Take-Helping-Others-Success/dp/0143124986
15. https://www.amazon.com/Happiness-Advantage-Principles-Psychology-Performance/dp/0307591549
16. https://www.amazon.com/Willpower-Doesnt-Work-Discover-Success/dp/0316441325
17. https://www.bluezones.com/blue-zones-of-happiness/
18. http://web.a.ebscohost.com/ehost/detail/detail?vid=13&sid=cf577dfd-426c-4ef0-bc51-462ca72c48b9%40sessionmgr4007&bdata=JnNpdGU9ZWhvc3QtbGl2ZQ%3d%3d#AN=12020791&db=buh

19. https://leanstack.com/
20. https://www.amazon.com/Running-Lean-Iterate-Plan-Works/dp/1449305172
21. http://web.a.ebscohost.com/ehost/pdfviewer/pdfviewer?vid=10&sid=e45b2205-052b-4336-8632-9a4bdfb246d9%40sessionmgr4010
22. https://www.amazon.com/Mastering-Fear-Harnessing-Excellence-Relationships/dp/1632650118
23. https://www.coursera.org/learn/learning-how-to-learn
24. https://www.amazon.com/Peak-Secrets-New-Science-Expertise-ebook/dp/B011H56MKS

100% of the net proceeds from this book go to the Diana Spencer Foundation for Entrepreneurship.

www.ingramcontent.com/pod-product-compliance
Lightning Source LLC
Chambersburg PA
CBHW062344220526
45469CB00008B/2827